Rasmus Björn Anderson

America not Discovered by Columbus

A Historical Sketch of the Discovery of America by the Norsemen

Rasmus Björn Anderson

America not Discovered by Columbus
A Historical Sketch of the Discovery of America by the Norsemen

ISBN/EAN: 9783337010980

Printed in Europe, USA, Canada, Australia, Japan

Cover: Foto ©ninafisch / pixelio.de

More available books at **www.hansebooks.com**

America not Discovered by Columbus.

A Historical Sketch

of the

𝔇iscovery of 𝔄merica by the 𝔑orsemen,

IN THE TENTH CENTURY.

By R. B. ANDERSON, A.M.,

Of the University of Wisconsin.

With an Appendix

ON THE

HISTORICAL, LINGUISTIC, LITERARY AND SCIENTIFIC VALUE
OF THE SCANDINAVIAN LANGUAGES.

CHICAGO:
S. C. GRIGGS AND COMPANY.
LONDON: TRÜBNER & CO.
1874.

Entered according to Act of Congress, in the year 1874, by

S. C. GRIGGS AND COMPANY,

in the office of the Librarian of Congress, at Washington.

TO

STEPHEN H. CARPENTER, LL.D.,
PROFESSOR OF LOGIC, RHETORIC AND ENGLISH LITERATURE,

WHOSE FRIENDSHIP AND SYMPATHY HAVE BEEN A COMFORT
TO ME IN THE LINE OF STUDIES THAT
I HAVE PURSUED,
AND WHOSE VOICE HAS WHISPERED "COURAGE" WHEN-
EVER I SEEMED TO FALTER IN DESPAIR,

THE FOLLOWING PAGES ARE

RESPECTFULLY DEDICATED,

AS A TRIBUTE OF GRATITUDE AND AFFECTION, BY

THE AUTHOR.

PREFACE.

IN preparing this sketch, the author has freely made use of such material as he considered valuable for his purpose from the works of Torfæus, C. C. Rafn, J. T. Smith, N. L. Beamish, G. Gravier, B. F. De Costa, A. Davis, William and Mary Howitt, R. M. Ballantyne, P. A. Munch, R. Keyser, and others, and he is under special obligations to Dr. S. H. Carpenter, of the University of Wisconsin, for valuable suggestions.

This sketch does not claim to be without faults. The style may seem dull and heavy, but it is hoped that the reader will be generous in criticising an author who now makes his first appearance before the *American* public. The object of this sketch has been to present a readable and truthful narrative of the Norse discovery of America, to create some interest in the people, the literature, and the early institutions of Norway, and especially in Iceland,—that lonely and weird island,—the Ultima Thule of the Greek Philosophers; and of the good or ill performance of the task, a generous public must be the judge.

R. B. ANDERSON.

University of Wisconsin,
June 18, 1874.

CONTENTS.

CHAPTER I.
THE NORSEMEN, AND OTHER PEOPLES, INTERESTED IN THE DISCOVERY OF AMERICA, - - - - - 9

CHAPTER II.
NORSE LITERATURE HAS BEEN NEGLECTED BY THE LEARNED MEN OF THE GREAT NATIONS, - - - 15

CHAPTER III.
ANTIQUITY OF AMERICA, - - - - - - - 20

CHAPTER IV.
PHENICIAN, GREEK, IRISH, AND WELSH CLAIMS, - - 22

CHAPTER V.
WHO WERE THE NORSEMEN? - - - - - - 24

CHAPTER VI.
ICELAND, - - - - - - - - - - 28

CHAPTER VII.
GREENLAND, - - - - - - - - - 35

CHAPTER VIII.
THE SHIPS OF THE NORSEMEN, - - - - - 38

CHAPTER IX.
The Sagas and Documents are Genuine, - - - 41

CHAPTER X.
Bjarne Herjulfson, 986, - - - - - - - 45

CHAPTER XI.
Leif Erikson, 1000, - - - - - - - - 48

CHAPTER XII.
Thorwald Erikson, 1002, - - - - - - - 52

CHAPTER XIII.
Thorstein Erikson, 1005, - - - - - - - 56

CHAPTER XIV.
Thorfinn Karlsefne and Gudrid, 1007, - - - 57

CHAPTER XV.
The Discovery of America by Columbus, - - - 63

CHAPTER XVI.
Other Expeditions by the Norsemen, - - - - 65

CHAPTER XVII.
Conclusion, - - - - - - - - - 74

APPENDIX.
The Scandinavian Languages, - - - - - - 77.

CHAPTER I.

THE NORSEMEN, AND OTHER PEOPLES, INTERESTED IN THE DISCOVERY OF AMERICA.

THE object of the following pages is to present the reader with a brief account of the discovery of, early voyages to, and settlements in the Western Continent by the Norsemen, and to prove that Columbus must have had knowledge of this discovery by the Norsemen before he started to find America; and the author will not be surprised, if, in these pages, he should happen to throw out some thoughts which will conflict with the reader's previously-formed convictions about matters and things generally, and about historical facts especially.

The interest manifested by the reader of history is always greater the nearer the history which he reads is connected with his own country or with his own ancestors.

The American student, on the one hand, loves

to gaze upon the pages of American history. He admires the resolution, the fortitude and perseverance of the Pilgrim Fathers as they passed through their varied scenes of hardship and adversity when they made their first settlement upon our New England shores; and his whole soul is filled with transporting emotions of delight or sympathy as he reads the thrilling incidents of the sufferings and the victories of his countrymen who fought for his as well as for their own freedom during the Revolutionary war.

The Norse student, on the other hand, takes special pleasure in perusing the old Sagas and Eddas, and following the Vikings on their daring but victorious expeditions through European waters; and he draws inspiration from those beautiful and poetical ancient myths and stories about Odin, Thor, Baldur, Loke, the Giant Ymer, Ragnarokr, Yggdrasil, and that innumerable host of godlike heroes that illuminate the pages of his people's ancient history, and glitter like brilliant diamonds in the dust and darkness of bygone ages.

The subject to which your attention is invited,

the discovery of America, is, if properly presented, of equal interest to Americans and Norsemen. For those who are born and brought up on the fertile soil of Columbia, under the shady branches of the noble tree of American liberty, where the banner of progress and education is unfurled to the breeze, must naturally feel a deep interest in whatever facts may be presented in relation to the first discovery and early settlement of this their native land; while those who first saw the sunlight beaming among the rugged, snow-capped mountains of old Norway, and can still feel any of the heroic blood of their dauntless forefathers course its way through their veins, must, as a matter of course, feel an equally deep interest in learning that their own ancestors, the intrepid Norsemen, were the first pale-faced men who planted their feet on this gem of the ocean, and an interest too, I dare say, in having the claims of their native country to this honor vindicated.

The subject is not without special interest to the *Germans,* as it will appear in the course of this sketch that a German, who accompanied the Norsemen on their first expedition to this Western World, is intimately connected with the first name of this country; and there is no doubt that a German, through his writings about the Norsemen, was the means of bringing to Columbus valuable information about America.

The Welsh also have an interest in this subject; for it is generally believed, and not without reason, that their ancestors, under the leadership of Madoc, made a settlement in this country about the year 1170; thus, although they were 170 years later than the Norsemen in making the discovery, they were still 322 years ahead of Columbus, and Norsemen, therefore, claim in this question, Welshmen's sympathies against Columbus.

We might enlist the interest of Irishmen, too, in the presentation of this subject; for in the year 1029 (according to an account in the EYRBYGGJA SAGA, chapter 64), a Norse navigator, by name GUDLEIF GUDLAUGSON, undertook a voyage to Dublin, and on leaving Ireland again he intended to sail to Iceland; but he met with northeast winds and was driven far to the west and southwest in the sea, where no land was to be seen. It was already late in the summer, and Gudleif with his party made many prayers that they might escape from the sea. And it came to pass, says the Saga, that they saw land, but they knew not what land it was. Then they resolved to sail to the land, for they were weary with contending longer with the violence of the sea. They found there a good harbor, and when they had been a short time on shore, there came some people to them. They knew none of the people, but it "*rather appeared to them that they spoke Irish.*"

This portion of America, supposed to be situated south of the Chesapeake Bay, including NORTH and SOUTH CAROLINA, GEORGIA, and EAST FLORIDA, is in the Saga of THORFIN KARLSEFNE, chapter 13, called "*Irland edh Mykla,*" that is, *Great Ireland.* It is claimed that the name, *Great Ireland,* arose from the fact that the country had been colonized, long before *Gudlaugson's* visit, by the Irish, and that, they coming from their own green island to a vast continent possessing many of the fertile qualities of their own native soil, the appellation was natural and appropriate. There is nothing improbable in this conclusion; for the Irish, who visited and inhabited Iceland toward the close of the eighth century, to accomplish which they had to traverse a stormy ocean to the extent of eight hundred miles — who, as early as 725, were found upon the Faroe Isles — and whose voyages between Ireland and Iceland, in the tenth century, were of ordinary occurrence — a people so familiar with the sea were certainly capable of making a voyage across the Atlantic Ocean.

I cannot here enter upon any further discussion of the claims of the Irish, but you observe that this subject of discovering America cannot be treated exhaustively without bringing back to the mind fond recollections of the Emerald Isle, which was once the *School* of Western Europe, and her brave sons

"Inclyta gens hominum, milite, pace, fide,"

as Bishop Donatus somewhere has it.

CHAPTER II.

NORSE LITERATURE HAS BEEN NEGLECTED BY THE LEARNED MEN OF THE GREAT NATIONS.

ENLIGHTENED men all over the world are watching, with astonishment and admiration, the New World, from which great revolutions have proceeded, and in which great problems in human government, human progress and enterprise, are yet to be worked out and demonstrated.

People are everywhere eagerly observing every event that takes place in America, making it the subject of the most careful scrutiny, and the results, wonderful as they are, everywhere awaken the most intense interest. If you travel in England, in Germany, in Norway, or in any of the North-European countries, it is interesting to observe how familiar the common people are with matters and things pertaining to America. They not only know America better than they know their border countries, but there also are found not a few who keep themselves better posted on the affairs of America than on those of their own country.

Until recently it has generally been supposed that America was wholly unknown to European nations previous to the time of Columbus, but investigations by learned men have made it certain, beyond the shadow of a doubt, that the Europeans did have knowledge of this country long before the time of Columbus, and it has even been claimed, on quite plausible grounds, that some of the nations living here at the time of Columbus' discovery of this continent were descendants of Europeans.

As yet but few scholars have turned their attention to the North of Europe in relation to this subject, and hence the light which this extreme portion of the globe could give has hitherto been, in a great measure, neglected by the learned men of the great nations; and yet the antiquities of the North furnish a series of incontestable evidence that the coast of North America was discovered in the latter part of the tenth century, immediately after the discovery of Greenland by the Norsemen; furthermore, that this same coast was visited repeatedly by the Norsemen in the eleventh century; furthermore, that it was visited by them in the twelfth century; nay, also, that it was found again by them in the thirteenth century, and revisited in the fourteenth century. But even this is not all. These Northern antiquities also show that Christianity had been introduced in America not only among the Norsemen, who formed a settlement here, but also among the aborigines, or native population, that the Norsemen found here.

The learned men of the North are not to blame that this matter has not previously received due attention, for TORFÆUS published an account thereof as early as the year 1705, and besides him SUHM and SCHŒNING and LAGERBRING and WORMSKJOLD and SCHRŒDER, to say nothing of many others, have all presented the main facts in their historical works. But other nations paid no attention to all this. Not until 1837, when the celebrated Professor Rafn, through the laudable enterprise of the Royal Society of Northern Antiquities, published his learned, interesting and important work,* could scholars outside of Scandinavia be induced to examine the claims of the Norsemen. Professor Rafn succeeded, and he has perhaps done more than any other one man to call the attention of other nations to the importance of studying the Old Norse literature. Thus it is that scholars of other nations recently have begun to direct their attention to Northern Antiquities, Northern Languages and History. Germany and England, and I would like to add America, are now beginning to realize how much valuable material is to be found in these sources for elucidating the history and institutions of other contemporary nations; and especially do the early Sagas of the North throw much important light on the character of English and German institutions during the middle ages. The English and Germans are translating the Sagas as fast as they can. Professors KONRAD MAURER and TH. MOEBIUS are doing excellent work at their respective Universities in Germany; Oxford and Cambridge in England have each an Icelandic Professor, and three

---

* Antiquitates Americanæ, Hafniæ, 1837.

American Universities* give instruction in the Northern languages.

It is indeed an encouraging fact that these great nations are gradually becoming conscious of the importance of studying the Northern languages and literature, and we may safely hope that the time is not far distant when the Norsemen will be recognized in their right social, political, and literary character, and at the same time as navigators assume their true position in the pre-Columbian discovery of America.†

---

* CORNELL University in New York, and the MICHIGAN and WISCONSIN Universities.

† A step toward the vindication of the claims of the Norsemen to the honor of having discovered, settled, and made America known to the world, has been made, and a movement has been inaugurated for the erection of a monument in memory of the Norse navigator, LEIF ERIKSON, who visited and explored America in the year 1000, nearly five centuries before Columbus. For the realization of this object OLE BULL has contributed his eminent services. He has already given several concerts, both in this country and in Norway, the proceeds of which go to the monument fund. OLE BULL is President, Senator JOHN A. JOHNSON, Treasurer, and the writer of these pages Secretary, of the monument committee. Norway's famous poet and orator, BJÖRNSTJERNE BJÖRNSON (see Appendix), has promised to write, for the dedication of the monument, a cantata, to which the eminent Norse composer, EDWARD GRIEG, will write the music. BJÖRNSON has also promised to come to America in person and deliver the dedication oration.

CHAPTER III.

ANTIQUITY OF AMERICA.

BEFORE the plains of Europe rose above the primeval seas, the continent of America, according to Louis Agassiz, emerged from the watery waste that encircled the whole globe and became the scene of animal life. Hence the so-called New World is in reality the Old, and Agassiz gives abundant proof of its hoary age.

But who is able even to conjecture at what period it became the abode of man? Down to the close of the tenth century its written history is vague and uncertain. We can find traces of a rude civilization that suggest a very high antiquity. We can show mounds, monuments, and inscriptions, that point to periods, the contemplation of which would make Chronos himself grow giddy; yet among all these great and often impressive memorials there is no monument, mound, or inscription that solves satisfactorily the mystery of their origin. There are but few traditions even to aid us in our researches, and we can only infer that age after age nations and tribes have continued to rise into greatness and then fall and decline, and that barbarism and a rude culture have held alternate sway.*

---

* Compare De Costa, page 11.

CHAPTER IV.

PHENICIAN, GREEK, IRISH AND WELSH CLAIMS.

IN early times the Atlantic Ocean, like all other things without known bounds, was viewed by man with mixed feelings of fear and awe. It was usually called the Sea of Darkness.

Both PHENICIAN and TYRIAN voyages to the Western Continent, in early times, have been warmly advocated; and it is more than probable that the original inhabitants of the American continent crossed the Atlantic instead of piercing the icy regions of the north and coming by the way of Behring's Strait. From the Canaries, which were discovered and colonized by the Phenicians, it is a short voyage to America, and the bold sailors of the Mediterranean, after touching at these islands, could easily and safely be wafted to the western shore.

That the Greek philosopher, PYTHEAS, whose discoveries about the different length of the days in various climates appeared so astonishing to the other philosophers of his age, traversed the Atlantic Ocean about 340 years before Christ, can scarcely be doubted. He certainly discovered Thule* (Iceland), and determined its latitude, and we may at least say, that by this discovery he opened the way to America for the Norsemen.

Claims have been made, as I have already shown, both by the Irish and by the Welsh, that they crossed the Atlantic and found America before Columbus, but it is not my purpose to comment upon these claims in this short sketch. Much learned discussion has been devoted to the subject, but the early history of the American continent is still, to a great extent, veiled in mystery, and not until near the close of the tenth century of the present era can we point, with absolute certainty, to a genuine trans-Atlantic voyage.

---

* See Strabo's Geography, Book II, § 6.

CHAPTER V.

WHO WERE THE NORSEMEN?

THE first voyage to America, of which we have any perfectly reliable account, was performed by the NORSEMEN.

But who were the Norsemen? Permit me to answer this question briefly.

The Norsemen were the descendants of a branch of the Gothic race that, in early times, emigrated from Asia and traveled westward and northward, finally settling down in what is now the west central part of the kingdom of Norway. Their language was the Old Norse, which is still preserved and spoken in Iceland, and upon it are founded the modern Norse, Danish, and Swedish languages.

The ancient Norsemen were a bold and independent people. They were a free people. Their rulers were elected by the people in convention assembled, and all public matters of importance were decided in the assemblies, or open parliaments of the people.

Abroad they became the most daring adventurers. They made themselves known in every part of the civilized world by their daring as soldiers and navigators. They spread themselves along the shores of Europe, making conquests and planting colonies.

In their conquering expeditions they subdued a large portion of England, wrested Normandy, the fairest province of France, from the French king, conquered a considerable portion of Belgium, and made extensive inroads into Spain. Under Robert Guiscard they made themselves masters of Sicily and lower Italy in the eleventh century, and maintained their power there for a long time. During the Crusades they led the van of the chivalry of Europe in rescuing the Holy Sepulchre, and ruled over Antioch and Tiberias under Harald. They passed between the pillars of Hercules, they desolated the classic fields of Greece and penetrated the walls of Constantinople.

Straying away into the distant east, from where

they originally came, we find them laying the foundations of the Russian Empire, swinging their two-edged battle-axes in the streets of Constantinople, where they served as the leaders of the Greek Emperor's body-guard, and the main support of his tottering throne. They carved their mystic runes upon the marble lion* in the harbor of Athens in commemoration of their conquest of this city. The old Norse Vikings sailed up the rivers Rhine, Schelde, the Seine and Loire, conquering Cologne and Aachen, where they turned the emperor's palace into a stable, filling the heart of even the great Charlemagne with dismay.

The rulers of England are descendants of the Norsemen. Ganger Rolf, known in English history by the name Rollo, a son of Harald Haarfagr's friend, Ragnwald Mœrejarl, invaded France in the year 912 and took possession of Normandy; and in 1066, at the battle of Hastings, William the Conqueror, a great-grandson of Ganger Rolf, conquered England; and it is proper to add, that from this

---

* The marble lion upon which they carved their runes was afterwards taken to Venice and erected at the entrance of the arsenal, where it may be seen at the present time.

conquest the pride and glory of Great Britain descended.

It is also a noticeable fact, that the most serious opposition that William the Conqueror met with came from colonists of his own race, who had settled in Northumbria. He wasted their lands with fire and sword, and drove them beyond the border; but still we find their energy, their perseverance and their speech existing in the north English and lowland Scotch dialects.

CHAPTER VI.

ICELAND.

BUT Europe did not set bounds to the voyages and enterprises of the Norsemen. In the year 860 they discovered Iceland, and soon afterwards established upon this island a republic, which flourished four hundred years. The Icelandic republic furnishes the very best evidence of the independent spirit which characterized the Norsemen.

Political circumstances* in Norway urged many of the boldest and most independent people in the country to seek an asylum of freedom. HARALD HAARFAGR (*i. e.* the Fair-haired) had determined to make himself monarch of all Norway. He was instigated to unite Norway under his scepter by the ambition of the fair and proud RAGNA ADILS- DATTER (daughter), whom he loved and courted; but she declared that the man she married would have to be king of all Norway. Harald accepted the conditions; and after twelve years' hard fighting, during which time he neither cut nor combed his hair once,* in the year 872, at the battle of Hafrsfjord, Norway became united into one kingdom, instead of being divided into thirty-one small republics, as had been the case before that time.

Harald had subdued or slain the numerous leaders, and had passed a law abolishing all freehold tenure of property,† usurping it for the crown. To this the proud freemen of Norway would not submit. Disdaining to yield their ancient independence and be degraded, they resolved to leave those lands and homes, which they could now scarcely call their own, and set out with their families and followers in quest of new seats. There were as great emigrations from Norway in those days as there are now. The Norse spirit of enterprise is as old as their history.

Whither then should they go, was the question.

---

* He made a pledge to Ragna that he would neither cut nor comb his hair until he had subjugated all Norway.

† This so-called udal, [Icel. ódal, Norse odel, allodium,] *i. e.* independent tenure of property, was given back to the Norsemen by King Hakon the Good in the year 935, and has never since been taken away from them.

Some went to the Hebrides, others to the Orkney isles; some to the Shetland and Faroe isles; many went as Vikings to England, Scotland and France; but by far the greater number went to the more distant and therefore more secure Iceland, which had been discovered by the celebrated Norse Viking NADDODD in 860, and called by him Snowland; rediscovered by Gardar, of Swedish extraction in 864, after whom it was called Gardar's Holm (island), and visited by two Norsemen, Ingolfr and Leif (Hjoerleifr) in 870, by whom it was called Iceland. This emigration from Norway to Iceland began in the year 874, a thousand years ago this summer; and thus this strange island was peopled —and in a few years peopled to a surprising extent. It was not long before it had upwards of 50,000 inhabitants. You must bear in mind that this colonization was on an island in the cold North Sea, a little below the Arctic Circle. It was in a climate where grain refused to ripen, and where the people often were obliged to shake the snow off the frozen hay before they could carry it. Fishing, the main support of the people, was often obstructed by ice from the polar regions filling their harbors, and the whole island presented a most melancholy aspect of desolation. But still the people continued to flock thither and become attached to the soil. They were surrounded the whole year by dreary ice-mountains, the glare of volcanic flames, and the roaring of geysers or boiling springs. Still they loved this wild country, because they were *free;* and through the long winters, when the sun nearly or entirely disappeared from above the horizon, and nothing but northern lights flickered over their heads, they seemed only the more thrown upon their intellectual resources, and passed the time in reciting the Eddas and Sagas of their ancestors.

Perhaps I ought to beg your pardon for dwelling so long upon the subject of Iceland; but my apology is that, in the first place, Iceland is of itself an exceedingly interesting country; and, in the next place, it is really the *hinge upon which the door swings* which opened America to Europe. This island had been visited by Pytheas 340 years before Christ; and, according to the Irish monk DICUILUS, who wrote a geography in the year 825, it had been visited by some Irish priests in the summer of 795.* It was the settlement of Iceland by the Norsemen, and the constant voyages between this island and Norway, that led to the discovery, first of Greenland and then of America; and it is due to the high intellectual standing and fine historical taste of the Icelanders that records of these voyages were kept, first to instruct Columbus how to find America, and afterwards to solve for us the mysteries concerning the discovery of this continent.

Iceland is a small island, in the 65th deg. north latitude, of about 1,800 geographical square miles. Its valleys are almost without verdure, and its mountains without trees. Still, it contains, even at the present time, no less than 70,000 inhabitants, who live a peaceable and contented life, still clinging to their ancient language, and studying foreign languages, science, philosophy, and history, as we do who live in milder and more favored climes. Now, as in olden times, the earth trembles in the throes of the earthquake,—the geysers still spout their scalding water, and the plain belches forth mud,—

---

* *Vid.* Dicuilus, De Mensura Orbis Terræ, ed. Latronne, page 38.

while the grand old jokul,* Mount Hekla, clad in white robes of eternal snow, brandishes aloft its volcanic torch, as if threatening to set the very heavens on fire.

For ages Iceland was destined to become the sanctuary and preserver of the grand old literature of the North. Paganism prevailed there more than a century after the island became inhabited; the old traditions were cherished and committed to memory, and shortly after the introduction of Christianity the Old Norse literature was put in writing.

The ancient literature and traditions of Iceland excel anything of their kind in Europe during the middle ages. The Icelandic poems have no parallel in all the treasures of ancient literature. There are gigantic proportions about them, and great and overwhelming tragedies in them, which rival those of Greece. The early literature of Iceland is now fast becoming recognized as equal to that of ancient Greece and Rome.

The original Teutonic life lived longer and more independently in Norway, and especially in Iceland,

---

* Mountains covered with perpetual snow are called "jökuls" in Iceland.

than elsewhere, and had more favorable opportunities to grow and mature; and the Icelandic literature is the full-blown flower of the Teutonic heathendom. This Teutonic heathendom, with its beautiful and poetical mythology, was rooted out by superstitious priests in Germany, and the other countries inhabited by Teutonic peoples, before it had developed sufficiently to produce blossoms, excepting in England, where a kindred branch of the Gothic race rose to eminence in letters, and produced the Anglo-Saxon literature.

CHAPTER VII.

GREENLAND.

BUT, as time passed on, the people of Iceland felt a new impulse for colonizing new and strange lands, and the tide of emigration began to tend with irresistible force toward Greenland, in the west, which country also became settled in spite of its wretched climate.

The discovery of Greenland was a natural consequence of the settlement of Iceland, just as the discovery of America afterwards was a natural consequence of the settlement of Greenland. Between the western part of Iceland and the eastern part of Greenland there is a distance of only forty-five geographical miles. Hence, some of the ships that sailed to Iceland, at the time of the settlement of this island and later, could in case of a violent east wind, which is no rare occurrence in those regions, scarcely avoid approaching the coast of Greenland sufficiently to catch a glimpse of its jokuls,—nay, even to land on its islands and promontories., Thus it is said that Gunnbjorn, Ulf Krage's son, saw land lying in the ocean at the west of Iceland, when, in the year 876, he was driven out to the sea by a storm. Similar reports were heard, from time to time, by other mariners. About a century later a certain man, by name ERIK THE RED, had fled from Jaedern, in Norway, on account of manslaughter, and had settled in the western part of Iceland. Here he also was outlawed for manslaughter, by the public assembly, and condemned to banishment. He therefore fitted out his ship, and resolved to go in search of the land in the west that Gunnbjorn and others had seen. He set sail in the year 984, and found the land as he had expected, and remained there exploring the country for two years. At the end of this period he returned to Iceland, giving the newly-discovered country the name of GREENLAND, in order, as he said, to attract settlers, who would be favorably impressed with so pleasing a name.

The result was that many Icelanders and Norsemen emigrated to Greenland, and a flourishing colony was established, with GARDAR for its capital city, which, in the year 1261, became subject to the crown of Norway. The Greenland colony maintained its connection with the mother countries for a period of no less than 400 years; yet it finally disappeared, and was almost forgotten. Torfæus gives a list of seventeen bishops who ruled in Greenland.

CHAPTER VIII.

THE SHIPS OF THE NORSEMEN.

BEFORE following the Norsemen further on their westward course, it may not be out of place to say a few words about their ships. Having crossed the briny deep four times myself I have seen something of what is required in order to venture with safety on so long watery journeys. I have also seen one of the old Norse Viking ships, which is preserved at the University of Norway, and it seemed to me an excellent one both in respect to form and size. Now, I do not mean to say that the old Norsemen possessed such ocean crafts as now plow the deep between New York and Liverpool; but what I mean to say is this, that the Norsemen were then, as they are now, very excellent navigators. They had good sea-going vessels, some of which were of large size. We have an account, in Olaf Tryggvason's Saga, of one that was in many respects remarkable. That part of the keel which rested on the ground was 140 feet long. None but the choicest material was used in its construction. It contained thirty-four rowing-benches, and its stem and stern were overlaid with gold.* Their vessels would compare favorably with those of other nations, which have been used in later times in expeditions around the world, and were in every way adapted for an ocean voyage. They certainly were as well fitted to cross the Atlantic as were the ships of Columbus. From the Sagas we also learn that the Norsemen fully understood the importance of cultivating the study of navigation; they knew how to calculate the course of the sun and moon, and how to measure time by the stars. Without a high degree of nautical knowledge they could never have accomplished their voy-

---

* This ship of Olaf Tryggvason was called the *Long* Serpent, and was built by the ship-carpenter Thorberg, who is celebrated in the annals of the North for his ship-building. The Earl Hakon had a dragon containing forty rowing-benches. King Canute had one containing sixty, and King Olaf, the saint, possessed two ships capable of carrying two hundred men each. The Norse dragons glided on the waters as gracefully as ducks or swans, of which they also had the form. Compare also "Saga Frithjofs ens Frœkna," chapter 1, where his good ship Ellida is described.

ages to England, France, Spain, Sicily, Greece, and those still more difficult voyages to Iceland and Greenland.

I have now given a brief historical sketch of the voyages and enterprises of the Norsemen. I have done this to show that they were capable of the exploit of discovering America — nay, that it was in fact an unavoidable result of their constant seafaring life; so that even if we did not have the unmistakable language of the Sagas, we might still be able to assert, with a considerable degree of certainty, that the Norsemen must have been aware of the existence of the American continent. Yes, the Norsemen were truly a great people! Their spirit found its way into the Magna Charta* of England and into the Declaration of Independence in America. The spirit of the Vikings still survives in the bosoms of Englishmen, Americans and Norsemen, extending their commerce, taking bold positions against tyranny, and producing wonderful internal improvements in these countries.

---

* Compáre William and Mary Howitt.

CHAPTER IX.

THE SAGAS AND DOCUMENTS ARE GENUINE.

WE have now seen that the Norsemen made themselves known in every part of the civilized world; that they had excellent ships, that they were well trained seamen, and a highly civilized nation, possessing in fact all the means necessary for reaching the continent in the west; and we are thus prepared for the vital question, Did the Norsemen actually discover and explore the coast of the country now known as America? There is certainly no improbability in the idea. Open an atlas at the map of the Atlantic Ocean, or at the maps of the two hemispheres. Observe the distance between Norway and Iceland, and the distances between Iceland and Greenland, and Greenland and Newfoundland. You perceive it is more than twice the distance between Norway and Iceland that it is between Iceland and Greenland, and not far from twice the distance that it is between Greenland and Labrador, and thence on to Newfoundland. Now, after conceding the fact that Norse colonies existed in Greenland for at least three hundred years, which every student of Norse history knows to be a fact, we must prepare ourselves for the proposition that America was discovered by the Norsemen. It would be altogether unreasonable to suppose that a seafaring people like the Norsemen, who traversed the broad western ocean to reach Iceland and Greenland, could live for three centuries within a short voyage of this vast continent and never become aware of its existence.

But fortunately on this point we are not left to conjecture. We have a complete written record of the discovery. Intelligent men must first succeed in blotting out innumerable pages of well authenticated history, before they undertake to deny or dispute the facts of this discovery. While literary darkness overspread the whole of the European continent for many centuries following the tenth, letters were highly cultivated in Iceland; and this is the very time and country in which the Sagas containing a record of the discovery of America originated. That they were written long before Columbus, is as easy to demonstrate as the fact that Herodotus wrote his history before the era of Christ. The authenticity and authority of the Icelandic Sagas has been fully acknowledged by ALEXANDER VON HUMBOLDT in his Cosmos,* by MALTE-BRUN,† and many other distinguished scholars; and therefore a further discussion is at this time unnecessary on this point.

---

* Cosmos, Vol. II., pages 269-272, where Alexander von Humboldt, discussing the pre-Columbian discovery of America by the Norsemen, says: "We are here on historical ground. By the critical and highly praiseworthy efforts of Professor Rafn and the Royal Society of Northern Antiquaries in Copenhagen, the Sagas and documents in regard to the expeditions of the Norsemen to Helluland (Newfoundland), to Markland (the mouth of the St. Lawrence river and Nova Scotia), and to Vinland (Massachusetts) have been published and satisfactorily commented upon. * * * The discovery of the northern part of America by the Norsemen cannot be disputed. The length of the voyage, the direction in which they sailed, the time of the sun's rising and setting, are accurately given. While the Chalifat of Bagdad was still flourishing under the Abbasides, and while the rule of the Samanides, so favorable to poetry, still flourished in Persia, America was discovered, about the year 1000, by Leif, son of Erik the Red, at about 41½° N. L."

† Vid. Nouvelles annales des voyages, de la géographie, de l'histoire et de l'archéologie, rédigées par M. V.-A. MALTE-BRUN, secrétaire de la commission centrale de la société de géographie de Paris, member de plusieurs sociétés savantes. Août, 1858, pag. 253.

The manuscripts, in which we have the Sagas relating to America are found in the celebrated CODEX FLATŒENSIS, a skin-book that was finished in the year 1387. This work, written with great care and executed in the highest style of art, is now preserved in its integrity in the archives of Copenhagen, and a carefully printed copy* of it is to be found in Mimer's library at the University of Wisconsin. We gather from this work, that the Norsemen, after discovering and settling Greenland, and then keeping a bold southwestern course, discovered America more than 500 years before Columbus; and I shall in the following chapters present some of the main circumstances of this discovery.

---

* FLATEYARBOK, Christiania (Norway), 1860–1868.

CHAPTER X.

BJARNE HERJULFSON, 986.

IN the year 986, the same year that he returned from Greenland, the above-named ERIK THE RED moved from Iceland to Greenland, and among his numerous friends, who accompanied him, was an Icelander by name HERJULF.

Herjulf had a son by name BJARNE, who was a man of enterprise and fond of going abroad, and who possessed a merchant-ship, with which he gathered wealth and reputation. He used to be by turns a year abroad and a year at home with his father. He chanced to be away in Norway when his father moved over to Greenland, and on returning to Iceland he was so much disappointed on hearing of his father's departure with Erik, that he would not unload his ship, but resolved to follow his old custom and take up his abode with his father. "Who will go with me to Greenland?"

said he to his men. "We will all go with you," replied the men. "But we have none of us ever been on the Greenland Sea before," said Bjarne. "We mind not that," said the men,—so away they sailed for three days and lost sight of Iceland. Then the wind failed. After that a north wind and fog set in, and they knew not where they were sailing to. This lasted many days, until the sun at length appeared again, so that they could determine the quarters of the sky, and lo! in the horizon they saw, like a blue cloud, the outlines of an unknown land. They approached it. They saw that it was without mountains, was covered with wood, and that there were small hills inland. Bjarne saw that this did not answer to the description of Greenland; he knew he was too far south; so he left the land on the larboard side and sailed northward two days, when they got sight of land again. The men asked Bjarne if this was Greenland; but he said it was not, "For in Greenland," he said, "there are great snowy mountains; but this land is flat and covered with trees." They did not go ashore, but turning the bow from the land, they kept the sea with a fine breeze from the southwest for three days, when a third land was seen. Still Bjarne would not go ashore, for it was not like what had been reported of Greenland. So they sailed on, driven by a violent southwest wind, and after four days they reached a land which suited the description of Greenland. Bjarne was not deceived, for it was Greenland, and he happened to land close to the place where his father had settled.

It cannot be determined with certainty what parts of the American coast Bjarne saw; but from the circumstances of the voyage, the course of the winds, the direction of the currents, and the presumed distance between each sight of land, there is reason to believe that the first land that Bjarne saw in the year 986 was the present NANTUCKET, one degree south of Boston; the second NOVA SCOTIA, and the third NEWFOUNDLAND. Thus BJARNE HERJULFSON was the first *European* whose eyes beheld any part of the American continent.

CHAPTER XI.

LEIF ERIKSON, 1000.

WHEN Bjarne visited Norway, a few years later, and told of his adventure, he was censured in strong terms by Jarl (Earl) Erik and others, because he had manifested so little interest that he had not even gone ashore and explored these lands, and because he could give no more definite account of them. Still, what he did say was sufficient to arouse in the mind of LEIF ERIKSON, son of Erik the Red, a determination to solve the problem and find out what kind of lands these were that were talked so much about. He bought Bjarne's ship from him, set sail with a good crew of thirty-five men, and found the lands just as Bjarne had described them, far away to the southwest of Greenland. They landed in HELLULAND (NEWFOUNDLAND) and in MARKLAND (NOVA SCOTIA), explored these countries somewhat, gave them names, and proceeded from the latter into the open sea with a northeast wind, and were two days at sea before they saw land again. They sailed into a sound. It was very shallow at ebb-tide, so that their ship stood dry and there was a long way from their ship to the water. But so much did they desire to land that they did not give themselves time to wait until the water rose again under their ship, but ran at once on shore, at a place where a river flows out of a lake.* But as soon as the water rose up under the ship, they rowed out in their boats, floated the ship up the river and thence into the lake, where they cast anchor, brought their skin cots out of the ship, and raised their tents. After this they took counsel, and resolved to remain through the winter, and built a large house. There was no want of salmon, either in the river or in the lake, and larger salmon than they had before seen. The nature of the country was, as they thought, so good that cattle would not require house-feeding in winter. Day and night were more equal than in

---

* This lake is Mount Hope Bay. The tourist, in traveling that way by rail, will at first take Mount Hope Bay for a lake. B. F. DeCosta, page 32.

Greenland or Iceland, for on the shortest day the sun was above the horizon from half-past seven in the forenoon till half-past four in the afternoon; which circumstance gives for the latitude of the place 41° 24' 10"; hence Leif's booths are thought to have been situated at or near Fall River, Massachusetts. Leif Erikson called the country VINLAND, and the cause of this was the following interesting incident: There was a German in Leif Erikson's party by name TYRKER. He was a prisoner of war, but had become Leif's special favorite. He was missing one day after they came back from an exploring expedition. Leif Erikson became very anxious about Tyrker, and fearing that he might be killed by wild beasts or by Indians,* he went out with a few men to search for him. Toward evening he was found coming home, but in a very excited state of mind. The cause of his excitement was some fruit which he had found, and which he held up in his hands,

---

* Our Norse colonists in Vinland had frequent intercourse with the natives, whom they called "Skrællinger." This name is derived from the verb "skræla," which means to peel; hence skrælling (peeling) alludes to their small and shriveled aspect. Compare also the adjective "skral," which means slim, lean.

shouting: "Weintrauben! Weintrauben!! Weintrauben!!!" The sight and taste of this fruit, to which he had been accustomed in his own native land, had excited him to such an extent that he seemed drunk, and for some time he would do nothing but laugh, devour grapes and talk German, which language our Norse discoverers did not understand. At last he spoke Norse, and explained that he, to his great joy and surprise, had found vines and grapes in great abundance. From this circumstance the land got the name of VINLAND, and history got the interesting fact that a German was along with the daring argonauts of the Christian era.

Here is then a short account of the first expedition to America. It took place in the year 1000, and LEIF ERIKSON was the first pale-faced man who planted his feet on the American continent. Give Leif Erikson a place in history!

CHAPTER XII.

THORWALD ERIKSON, 1002.

IN the spring, when the winds were favorable, Leif Erikson returned to Greenland. The expedition to Vinland was much talked of, and THORWALD, Leif's brother, thought that the land had been much too little explored. Then said Leif to Thorwald: "You may go with my ship, brother, to Vinland, if you like." And so another expedition was fitted out, in the year 1002, by Thorwald Erikson, who went to Vinland and remained there three years; but it cost him his life, for in a battle with the Skrællings an arrow from one of the natives of America pierced his side, causing death. He was buried in Vinland, and two crosses were erected on his grave—one at his head and one at his feet. Hallowed ground this beneath whose sod rests the dust of the first Christian and the first European who died in America! His death and burial also gains interest in another respect, for in the year 1831 there was found in the vicinity of Fall River, Massachusetts, *a skeleton* in *armor,* and many of the circumstances connected with it are so wonderful that it might indeed seem almost as though it were the skeleton of this very Thorwald Erikson! This skeleton in armor attracted much attention at the time, was the subject of much learned discussion, and our celebrated poet Longfellow wrote, in the year 1841, a poem about it, beginning:

"**Speak! speak! thou fearful guest!**"

After which he makes the skeleton tell about his adventures as a viking, about the pine forests of Norway, about his voyage across the stormy deep, and about the discovery of America, concerning which he says:

"Three weeks we westward bore,
And when the storm was o'er,
Cloudlike we saw the shore
    Stretching to leeward;
There for my lady's bower
Built I the lofty tower,*
Which to this very hour
    Stands looking seaward."

---

* The tower here referred to is the famous Newport tower in Rhode Island, which undoubtedly was built by the Norsemen.

The following are the last two verses of the poem:

> "Still grew my bosom then,
> Still as a stagnant fen,
> Hateful to me were men,
>   The sunlight hateful!
> In the vast forest here,
> Clad in my warlike gear,
> Fell I upon my spear,
>   Oh, death was grateful!

> "Thus seamed with many scars,
> Bursting these prison bars,
> Up to its native stars,
>   My soul ascended.
> There from the flowing bowl
> Deep drinks the warrior's soul:
> Skaal! to the Northland, skaal!
>   Thus the tale ended."

The great Swedish chemist Berzelius analyzed* a part of the breastplate which was found on the

---

*A bronze article found in Denmark, and dating with certainty back to the tenth century, was also analyzed, and the annexed table shows the result of the analysis:

	Breastplate from America.	Bronze Article from Denmark.
Copper	70.29	67.13
Zinc	28.03	20.39
Tin	0.91	9.24
Lead	0.74	3.39
Iron	0.03	0.11

skeleton, and found that in composition it corresponded with metals used in the North during the tenth century; and comparing the Fall River breastplate with old northern armors, it was also found to correspond with these in style.

When the Norsemen had buried their chief, Thorwald, they returned to Leifsbudir (Leif's booths), loaded their ships with the products of the land and returned to Greenland in the year 1005.

CHAPTER XIII.

THORSTEIN ERIKSON, 1005.

THEN the Sagas tell us that THORSTEIN, the youngest son of Erik the Red, was seized with a strong desire to pass over to Vinland to fetch the body of his brother Thorwald. He was married to GUDRID, a woman remarkable for her beauty, her dignity, her prudence, and her good discourse. Thorstein fitted out a vessel, manned it with twenty-five men selected for their strength and stature, besides himself and Gudrid. When all was ready they put out to sea, and were soon out of sight of land. Through the whole summer they were tossed about on the deep and were driven they knew not whither. Finally they made land, which they found to be Lysefjord, on the western coast of Greenland. Here Thorstein and several of his men died, and Gudrid returned to Eriksfjord.

CHAPTER XIV.

THORFINN KARLSEFNE AND GUDRID, 1007.

THE most distinguished explorer of Vinland was THORFINN KARLSEFNE. He was a wealthy and influential man. He was descended from the most famous families in the North. Several of his ancestors had been elected kings. In the fall of 1006, he came from Norway to Eriksfjord with two ships. Karlsefne made rich presents to Leif Erikson, and Leif offered the Norse navigator the hospitalities of Brattahlid during winter. After the Yule festival Thorfinn began to treat with Leif as to the marriage of Gudrid, Leif being the person to whom the right of betrothment belonged. Leif gave a favorable ear to his advances, and in the course of the winter their nuptials were celebrated with due ceremony. The conversation frequently turned at Brattahlid upon Vinland the Good, many saying that an expedition thither held out fair prospects of gain. The result was that Thorfinn, accompanied by his wife, who urged him to the undertaking, sailed to Vinland in the spring of 1007, and remained there three years. The Sagas lay considerable stress upon the fact that Gudrid persuaded him to undertake this expedition. She also appears to have taken a prominent part in the whole enterprise. Imagine yourself way off in Greenland. Imagine Gudrid and Thorfinn Karlsefne taking a walk together on the sea-beach, and Gudrid talking to her husband in this wise:

"I wonder that you, Thorfinn, with good ships and many stout men, and plenty of means, should choose to remain in this barren spot instead of searching out the famous Vinland and making a settlement there. Just think what a splendid country it must be, and what a desirable change for all of us. Thick and leafy woods like those of old Norway, instead of these rugged cliffs and snow-clad hills. Fields of waving grass and rye instead of moss-covered rocks and sandy soil. Trees large enough to build houses and ships instead of willow bushes, that are fit for nothing except to save our cattle from starvation when the hay-crop runs out; besides longer sunshine in winter, and more genial warmth all the year round, instead of howling winds and ice and snow. Truly I think this country has been wofully misnamed when they called it Greenland."

You can easily imagine that Thorfinn was convinced by such persuasive arguments, and he resolved to follow his wife's advice.

The expedition which now set out for Vinland was on a much larger scale than any of the expeditions that had preceded it. That Leif and Thorwald and Thorstein had not intended to make their permanent abode in Vinland was plain, from the fact that they brought neither women nor flocks nor herds with them. Karlsefne, on the other hand, went forth fully equipped for colonization. The party consisted of *one hundred and fifty-one* men and seven women. A number of cattle and sheep were also carried on this occasion to Vinland. They all arrived there in safety, and remained, as has been stated, three years, when hostilities between them and the Skrællings compelled them to give up their colony.

The Saga gives a very full account of Thorfinn's enterprises in Vinland; about the traffic with the Skrællings; about the development of the colony, etc.; all of which I am compelled to omit in this sketch. I must call attention, however, to the interesting fact that a son was born to Thorfinn and Gudrid the year after they had established themselves in their quarters at Straumfjord (Buzzard's Bay). His name was SNORRE THORFINNSON. He was born in the present State of Massachusetts, in the year 1008, and he was the first man of European blood of whose birth in America we have any record. From him the famous sculptor, Albert Thorwaldsen, is lineally descended, besides a long train of learned and distinguished men, who have flourished during the last eight centuries in Iceland and Denmark.

In the next place, attention is invited to an inscription on a rock, situated on the right bank of the Taunton river, in Bristol county, Massachusetts. It is familiarly called the DIGHTON WRITING ROCK INSCRIPTION. It stands in the very region which the Norsemen frequented. It is written in characters which the natives have never used nor sculptured. This inscription was copied by Dr. Danforth as early as 1680, by Cotton Mather in 1712; it was copied by Dr. Greenwood in 1730, by Stephen Sewell in 1768, by James Winthrop in 1788, and has been copied at least four times in the present century. The rock was seen and talked of by the first settlers in New England, long before anything was said about the Norsemen discovering America before Columbus.

Near the center of the inscription we read distinctly, in Roman characters,

CXXXI,

which is 151,* the exact number of Thorfinn's party. Then we find an N, a boat, and the Runic character for M, which may be interpreted "N(orse) seafaring M(en)." Besides we have the word NAM—took (took possession), and the whole of Thorfinn's name, with the exception of the first letter. Repeating these characters we have

ORFIN, CXXXI, N ⛵ M, NAM,

---

* The Icelanders reckoned twelve decades to the hundred, and called it stort hundrad (great hundred).

which has been interpreted by Prof. Rafn as follows: "Thorfin, with one hundred and fifty-one Norse seafaring men took possession of this land (landnam)."

In the lower left corner of the inscription is a figure of a woman and a child, near the latter of which is the letter S, reminding us most forcibly of Gudrid and her son, Snorre. Upon the whole the Dighton Writing Rock removes all doubt concerning the presence of Thorfinn Karlsefne and the Norsemen at Taunton river, in the beginning of the eleventh century.

CHAPTER XV.

OTHER EXPEDITIONS BY THE NORSEMEN.

THE Sagas give elaborate accounts of other expeditions by the Norsemen to Vinland. Thus there is one by Freydis in the year 1011; and in the year 1121 the Bishop Erik Upsi went as a missionary to Vinland.

Then there are Sagas that give accounts of expeditions by Norsemen to GREAT IRLAND (North and South Carolina, Georgia and Florida), but I will omit these in the present sketch.

The last expedition mentioned was in the year 1347, but this was in the time of the Black Plague, which raged throughout Europe with unrelenting fury from 1347 to 1351, and also reached Iceland, Greenland and Vinland, and cut off communication between these countries. The Black Plague reduced the population of Norway alone from two millions to three hundred thousand, and this fact gives us some idea of the terrible ravages of this fearful epidemic. It is evident that the Black Plague left no surplus population for expeditions to America or elsewhere.

CHAPTER XVI.

THE DISCOVERY OF AMERICA BY COLUMBUS.

I WILL now devote a few pages to pointing out some of the threads that connect this discovery of America by the Norsemen with the more recent and better-known discovery by Columbus.

1. From a letter which Columbus himself wrote, and which we find quoted in Washington Irving's *Columbus*,* we know positively that while the design of attempting the discovery in the west was maturing in the mind of Columbus, he made a voyage to the north of Europe, and visited Iceland. This was in February, 1477, and in his conversation with the Bishop and other learned men of Iceland, he must have been informed of the extraordinary fact, that their countrymen had discovered a great country beyond the western ocean, which seemed to extend southward to a great distance. This was

---

* Vol. I, page 59.

a circumstance not likely to rest quietly in the active and speculative mind of the great geographer and navigator. The reader will observe that, when Columbus was in Iceland, in the year 1477, fifteen years before he discovered America, only one hundred and thirty years had elapsed since the last Norse expedition to Vinland. There were undoubtedly people still living whose grandfathers had crossed the Atlantic, and it would be altogether unreasonable to suppose that he, who was constantly studying and talking about geography and navigation, possibly could visit Iceland and not hear anything of the land in the west.

2. Gudrid, the wife of Thorfinn and mother of Snorre, made a pilgrimage to Rome after the death of her husband. It is related that she was well received, and she certainly must have talked there of her ever memorable trans-oceanic voyage to Vinland, and her three years' residence there. Rome paid much attention to geographical discoveries, and took pains to collect all new charts and reports that were brought there. Every new discovery was an aggrandizement of the papal dominion, a

new field for the preaching of the Gospel. The Romans might have heard of Vinland before, but she brought personal evidence.

3. That Vinland was known at the Vatican is clearly proved by the fact that the Pope Paschal II, in the year 1112, appointed Erik Upsi, Bishop of Iceland, Greenland and VINLAND, and Erik Upsi went personally to Vinland in the year 1121.

4. Recent developments in relation to Columbus tend to prove that he had opportunity to see a map of Vinland, procured from the Vatican for the Pinzons, and it would indeed astonish us more to learn that he, with his nautical knowledge, did not hear of America than that he did. We must also bear in mind that Columbus lived in an age of discovery; England, France, Portugal and Spain were vying with each other in discovering new lands and extending their territories.

5. But in addition to the SAGAS, the DIGHTON WRITING ROCK, the NEWPORT TOWER (which the Indians told the early New England settlers was built by the giants, and the Norse discoverers certainly looked like giants to the Indians, since the

former called the latter Skrællings), and in addition to the SKELETON IN ARMOR, we have a remarkable record of the early discovery of America by the Norsemen in the writings of ADAM OF BREMEN, a canon and historian of high authority, who died in the year 1076. He visited the Danish king Svend Esthridson, a nephew of Canute the Great, and on his return home he wrote a book "*On the Propagation of the Christian Religion in the North of Europe,*" and at the end of this book he added a geographical treatise "*On the Position of Denmark and other regions beyond Denmark.*" Having given an account of Denmark, Sweden, Norway, Iceland and Greenland, he says that, "*besides these there is still another region, which has been visited by many, lying in that ocean (the Atlantic), which is called* VINLAND, *because vines grow there spontaneously, producing very good wine; corn likewise springs up there without being sown;*" and as Adam of Bremen closes his account of Vinland he adds these remarkable words: "*This we know not by fabulous conjecture, but from positive statements of the Danes.*"

Now, Adam of Bremen's work was first published in the year 1073, and was read by intelligent men throughout Europe; and Columbus, being an educated man, and so deeply interested in geographical studies, especially when they treated of the Atlantic Ocean, could he be ignorant of so important a work?

I have here given *five* reasons why Columbus must have known the existence of the American continent before he started on his voyage of discovery. 1. Gudrid's visit to Rome. 2. The appointment, by Pope Paschal II, of Erik Upsi as Bishop of Vinland. 3. Adam of Bremen's account of Vinland in his book published in 1073. 4. The map procured from the Vatican for the Pinzons, which fact I have not, however, yet been able to establish with absolute certainty; and, 5, which caps the climax, Columbus's own visit to Iceland in the year 1477.

These are stubborn facts, and, if you read the biography of Columbus, you will find that he always maintained a firm conviction that there was land in the west. He says himself that he based this conviction on the authority of the *learned writers*.

He stated, before he left Spain, that he expected to find land soon after sailing about seven hundred leagues; hence he knew the breadth of the ocean, and must therefore have had a pretty definite knowledge of the situation of Vinland and Great Ireland. A day or two before coming in sight of the new world, he capitulated with his mutinous crew, promising, if he did not discover land within three days, to abandon the voyage. In fact the whole history of his discovery proves that he either must have possessed previous knowledge of America, or, as some have had the audacity to maintain, been inspired. We do not believe in that sort of inspiration. It makes Columbus a greater man, in our estimation, that he formed his opinion by a chain of logical deductions based upon thorough study and research. It is to the credit of Columbus, we say, that he investigated the nature of things; that he diligently searched the learned writers; that he paid close attention to all reports of navigators, and gathered up all those scattered gleams of knowledge that fell ineffectually upon ordinary minds. Washington Irving says: "When Columbus had formed his theory, it became fixed in his mind with singular firmness. He never spoke in doubt or hesitation, but with as much certainty as if his eyes had already beheld the promised land." We say, if he held this firm conviction on only presumptive evidence, then, with all due respect for his distinguished biographer, he is not entitled to the enviable reputation for scholarship and good judgment that has been accredited to him by Washington Irving. We claim to be vindicating the great name of Columbus, by showing that he must have based his *certainty* upon *equally certain* facts, which he possessed the ability and patience to study out, and the keenness of intellect to put together, and this gives *historical importance* to the discovery of America by the *Norsemen*. The fault that we find with Columbus is, that he was not honest and frank enough to tell where and how he had obtained his previous information about the lands which he pretended to discover; that he sometimes talked of himself as chosen by Heaven to make this discovery, and that he made the fruits of his labors subservient to the dominion of inquisition.

If our theory, then, does not make Columbus out as true and good a man as the reader may have considered him, we still insist that it proves him a man of extraordinary ability. It shows that he discovered America by study and research, and not by accident or inspiration. Care should always be taken to vindicate great names from accident or inspiration. It defeats one of the most salutary purposes of history and biography which is to furnish examples of what human genius and laudable enterprise can accomplish.

That the Spanish and more recent colonies in America could become more permanent than the Norse colonies, is chiefly to be attributed to the superiority that fire-arms gave the Europeans over the natives. The Norsemen had no fire-arms, and their higher culture could not defend them against the swarms of savages that attacked them. In the next place, the Black Plague reduced the population of Norway and Iceland beyond the necessity or even possibility to emigrate. If the communication between Vinland and the North could have been maintained say one hundred years longer, that is to the middle of the fifteenth century, it is difficult to determine what the result would have been. Possibly this sketch would have appeared in *Icelandic* instead of English. Undoubtedly the Norse colonies would have become firmly rooted by that time, and Norse language, nationality, and institutions might have played as conspicuous a part in America as the English and their posterity do now-a-days.

CHAPTER XVII.

CONCLUSION.

BUT it is not within the scope of this sketch to discuss this subject any further. Let us remember LEIF ERIKSON, the first white man who planted his feet on American soil! Let us remember his brother, THORWALD ERIKSON, the first European and the first Christian who was buried beneath American sod! Let us not forget THORFINN and GUDRID, who established the first European colony in America! nor their little son, SNORRE, the first man of European blood whose birthplace was in the New World! Let us erect a monument to Leif Erikson worthy of the man and the cause; and while the knowledge of this discovery of America lay for a long time hid in the unstudied literature of Iceland, let us take this lesson, that *"truth crushed to earth will rise again;"* that truth may often lie darkened and hid for a long time, but that it is like the beam of light from a star in some far distant region of the universe — after thousands of years it reaches some heavenly body and gives it light.

In the language of Mr. Davis: "Let us praise Leif Erikson for his courage, let us applaud him for his zeal, let us respect him for his motives, for he was anxious to enlarge the boundaries of knowledge. He reached the wished for land,

> "'Where now the western sun
> O'er fields and floods,
> O'er every living soul
> Diffuseth glad repose.'

He opened to the view a broad region, where smiling hope invites successive generations from the old world.

"Such men as an Alexander, or a Tamerlane, conquer but to devastate countries. Discoverers add new regions of fertility and beauty to those already known.

"And are not the hardy adventurers, plowing the briny deep, more attractive than the troops of Alexander, or Napoleon, marching to conquer the world, with plumes waving in the gentle breeze, and with arms glittering in the sunbeams? Who can tell all the benefits that discoverers confer on mankind?

> "'To count them all demands a thousand tongues,
> A throat of brass and adamantine lungs.'"

THE SCANDINAVIAN LANGUAGES;

Their Historical, Linguistic, Literary and Scientific Value.

ELUCIDATED BY

QUOTATIONS FROM EMINENT AMERICAN, ENGLISH, GERMAN AND FRENCH SCHOLARS.

NOTICES OF THESE LANGUAGES BY

H. W. LONGFELLOW, GEORGE P. MARSH, SAMUEL LAING, ROBERT BUCHANAN, SCHLEGEL, MALLET, AND OTHERS.

SELECTED AND EDITED WITH A FEW NOTES

BY R. B. ANDERSON, A. M.
Of the University of Wisconsin.

WHAT SCHOLARS SAY

ABOUT THE

HISTORICAL, LINGUISTIC AND LITERARY VALUE

OF THE

SCANDINAVIAN LANGUAGES.

"Der är flagga på mast och den visar åt norr, och
i norr är den älskade jord;
jag vill följa de himmelska vindarnas gång, jag vill
styra tillbaka mot Nord."

—*Tegner.*

ENGLISH VERSION.

"There's the flag on the mast, and it points to the North,
And the North holds the land that I love,
I will steer back to northward, the heavenly course
Of the winds guiding sure from above."

VERY little attention has hitherto been given in this country to the study of Scandinavian history, languages and literatures. We think this branch of study would not be so much neglected, if it were more generally known, what an extensive source of intellectual pleasure it affords to the scholar who is acquainted with it. We hope, therefore, to serve a good cause by calling your attention to a few quotations from American, English, German and French scholars, who have given much time and attention to the above named subjects, in order that it may be known what they, who may justly be considered competent to judge, say of their importance.

I will add that I have not found a scholar, who has devoted himself to this field of study and research, that has not at the same time become an *enthusiastic* admirer of Scandinavian and particularly Icelandic history, languages, and literatures.

To scientific students it is sufficient to say, that a knowledge of the Scandinavian languages at once introduces them to several writers of great eminence in the scientific world. I will briefly mention a few.

HANS CHRISTIAN OERSTED won for himself one of the greatest names of the age. His discovery, in 1820, of electro-magnetism — the identity of electricity and magnetism — which he not only discovered, but demonstrated incontestably, placed him at once in the highest rank of physical philosophers, and has led to all the wonders of the electric telegraph. His great work, "The Soul of Nature," in which he promulgates his grand doctrine of the universe, abundantly repays a careful perusal.

CARL VON LINNE (Linnæus) is the polar star in botany. He was Professor at the University of Sweden, died in 1788, and is the founder of the established system of botany. As Linnæus is the father of botany, so BERZELIUS might be called the father of the present system of chemistry. He is one of the greatest ornaments of science. He devoted his whole life sedulously to the promotion and extension of his favorite science, and to him is the world indebted for the discovery of many new elementary principles and valuable chemical combinations now in general use. He filled the chair of Chemistry in the University of Stockholm for forty-two years, and died in 1848. SCHEELE, MICHAEL SARS, HANSTEEN, and several others, are men who have distinguished themselves by their labors in the field of science, natural history and astronomy. And now read the following quotations, which we have promised to present.

MR. NORTH LUDLOW BEAMISH says: "The national literature of Iceland holds a distinct and eminent position in the literature of Europe. In that remote and cheerless isle * * * * religion and learning took up their tranquil abode, before the south of Europe had yet emerged from the mental darkness, which followed the fall of the Roman Empire. There the unerring memories of the Skalds and Sagamen were the depositories of past events, which, handed down from age to age, in one unbroken line of historical tradition, were committed to writing on the introduction of Christianity, and now come before us with an internal evidence of their truth, which places them *amongst the highest order of historical records*.

"To investigate the origin of this remarkable advancement in mental culture, and trace the progressive steps by which Icelandic literature attained an eminence which even now imparts a lustre to that barren land, is an object of *interesting* and *instructive* inquiry.

"Among no other people of Europe can the conception and birth of historical literature be more clearly traced than amongst the people of Iceland. Here it can be shown how memory took root, and gave birth to narrative; how narrative multiplied and increased until it was committed to writing, and how the written relation eventually became sifted and arranged in chronological order."

Samuel Laing, Esq.—" All that men hope for of good government and future improvement in their physical and moral condition—all that civilized men enjoy at this day of civil, religious, and political liberty —the British constitution, representative legislature, the trial by jury, security of property, freedom of mind and person, the influence of public opinion over the conduct of public affairs, the Reformation, the liberty of the press, the spirit of the age,—all that is or has been of value to man in modern times as a member of society, either in Europe or in America, may be traced to the spark left burning upon our shores by the Norwegian barbarians.

"There seem no good grounds for the favorite and hackneyed course of all who have written on the origin of the British constitution and trial by jury, who unriddle a few dark phrases of Tacitus concerning the institutions of the ancient Germanic tribes, and trace up to that obscure source the origin of all political institutions connected with freedom in modern Europe. In the (Norwegian) Sagas we find, at a period immediately preceding the first traces of free institutions in our history, the rude but very vigorous demonstrations of similar institutions existing in great activity among those northern people, who were masters of the country under Canute the Great, who for two generations before his time had occupied and inhabited a very large portion of it, and of whom a branch under William of Normandy became its ultimate and permanent conquerors. It may be more classical to search in the pages of Tacitus for allusions to the customs of the tribes wandering in his day through the forests of Germany, which may bear some faint resemblance to modern institutions, or to what we fancy our modern institutions may have been in their infancy; but it seems more consistent with correct principles of historic research to look for the origin of our institutions at the nearest, not at the most remote, source; not at what existed 1,000 years before in the woods of Germany, among people whom we must believe upon supposition to have been the ancestors of the invaders from the north of the Elbe, who conquered England, and must again believe upon supposition, that when this people were conquered successively by the Danes and Normans, they imposed their own peculiar institutions upon their conquerors, instead of receiving institutions from them; but at what actually existed, when the first notice of assemblies for legislative purposes can be traced in English history among the conquerors of the country, a cognate people, long established by previous conquests in a large portion of it, who used, if not the same, at least a language common to both, and who had no occasion to borrow, from the conquered, institutions which were flourishing at the time in their mother country in much greater vigor. "It is in these (Norwegian) Sagas, not in Tacitus, that we have to look for the origin of the political institutions of England. The reference of all matters to the *legislative assemblies of the people* is one of the most striking facts in the Sagas.

"The Sagas, although composed by natives of Iceland,

are properly *Norwegian literature.* The events, persons, manners, language, belong to *Norway;* and they are productions, which like the works of Homer, of Shakespeare, and of Scott, are strongly stamped with nationality of character and incident.

"A portion of that attention, which has exhausted classic mythology, and which has too long dwelt in the Pantheons of Greece and Rome, and is wearied with fruitless efforts to learn something more, where, perhaps, nothing more is to be learned, may very profitably, and very successfully, be directed to the vast field of Gothic research. For we are Goths and the descendants of Goths—

> "'The men,
> Of earth's best blood, of titles manifold.'

And it well becomes us to ask, what has Zeus to do with the Brocken, Apollo with Effersberg, or Poseidon with the Northern Sea? The gods of our fathers were neither Jupiter, nor Saturn, nor Mercury, but Odin, Brage, or Eger. If we marvel at the pictures of heathen divinities as painted by classical hands, let us not forget, that our ancestors had deities of their own—gods as mighty in their attributes, as refined in their tastes, as heroic in their doings, as the gods worshiped in the Parthenon or talked about in the forum."

M. MALLET says: "History has not recorded the annals of a people who have occasioned greater, more sudden, or more numerous revolutions in Europe than the Scandinavians, or whose antiquities, at the same time, are so little known. Had, indeed, their emigrations been only like those sudden torrents of which all traces and remembrance are soon effaced, the indifference that has been shown to them would have been sufficiently justified by the barbarism they have been approached with. But, during those general inundations, the face of Europe underwent so total a change, and during the confusion they occasioned, such different establishments took place; new societies were formed, animated so entirely by the new spirit, that the history of our own manners and institutions ought necessarily to ascend back, and even dwell a considerable time upon a period which discovers to us their chief origin and source.

"But I ought not barely to assert this. Permit me to support the assertions by proof. For this purpose, let us briefly run over all the different revolutions, which this part of the world underwent, during the long course of ages which its history comprehends, in order to see what share the nations of the north have had in producing them. If we recur back to the remotest times, we observe a nation issuing step by step from the forests of Scythia, incessantly increasing and dividing to take possession of the uncultivated countries, which it met with in its progress. Very soon after, we see the same people, like a tree full of vigor, extending long branches over all Europe; we see them also carrying with them, wherever they came, from the borders of the Black Sea to the extremities of Spain, of Sicily, and of Greece, a religion simple and martial as themselves, a form of government dictated by good sense and liberty, a restless unconquered spirit, apt to take fire at the very mention of subjection and constraint, and a ferocious courage nourished by a savage and vagabond life. While the gentleness of the climate softened imperceptibly the ferocity of those who settled in the south, colonies of Egyptians and Phenicians mixing with them upon the coasts of Greece, and thence passing over to those of Italy, taught them at last to live in cities, to cultivate letters, arts and commerce. Thus their opinions, their customs and genius, were blended together, and new states were formed upon new plans. Rome, in the meantime arose, and at length carried all before her. In proportion as she increased in grandeur, she forgot her ancient manners, and destroyed, among the nations whom she overpowered, the original spirit with which they were animated. But this spirit continued unaltered in the colder countries of Europe, and maintained itself there like the independency of the inhabitants. Scarce could fifteen or sixteen centuries produce there any change in that spirit. There it renewed itself incessantly; for, during the whole of that long interval, new adventurers issuing continually from the original inexhaustible country, trod upon the heels of their fathers towards the north, and, being in their turn succeeded by new troops of followers, they. pushed one another forward like the waves of the sea. The northern countries, thus overstocked, and unable any longer to contain such restless inhabitants, equally greedy of glory and plunder, discharged at length upon the Roman Empire the weight that oppressed them. The barriers of the Empire, ill defended by a people whom prosperity had enervated, were borne down on all sides by torrents of victorious armies. We then see the conquerors introducing, among the nations they vanquished, viz. into the very bosom of slavery and sloth, that spirit of independence and equality, that elevation of soul, that taste for rural and military life, which both the one and the other had originally derived from the same common source, but which were then among the Romans breathing their last. Dispositions and principles so opposite, struggled long with forces sufficiently equal, but they united in the end, they coalesced together, and from their coalition sprung those principles and that spirit which governed afterwards almost all the states of Europe, and which, notwithstanding the differences of climate, of religion, and particular accidents, do visibly reign in them, and retain, to this day, more or less, the traces of their first common origin.

"It is easy to see, from this short sketch, how greatly the nations of the earth have influenced the different fates of Europe; and if it be worth while to trace its revolutions to their causes; if the illustration of its institutions, of its police, of its customs, of its manners, of its laws, be a subject of useful and interesting inquiry; it must be allowed, that the antiquities of the *north*, that is to say, everything which tends to make us acquainted with its ancient inhabitants, merits a share in the attention of thinking men. But to render this obvious by a particular example: is it not well known that the most flourishing and celebrated states of Europe owe originally to the northern nations whatever liberty they now enjoy, either in their constitution or in the spirit of their government? For although the Gothic form of government has been almost everywhere altered or abolished, have we not retained, in most things, the opinions, the customs, the manners which that government had a tendency to produce? Is not this, in fact, the principal source of that courage, of that aversion to slavery, of that empire of honor which characterized in general the European nations; and of that moderation, of that easiness of access, and peculiar attention to the rights of humanity, which so happily distinguish our sovereigns from the inaccessible and superb tyrants of Asia? The immense extent of the Roman Empire had rendered its constitution so despotic and military, many of its emperors were such ferocious monsters, its senate was become so mean-spirited and vile, that all elevation of sentiment, everything that was noble and manly, seems to have been forever vanished from their hearts and minds; insomuch that if all Europe had received the yoke of Rome in this her state of debasement, this fine part of the world reduced to the inglorious condition of the rest could not have avoided falling into that kind of barbarity, which is of all others the most incurable; as, by making as many slaves as there are men, it degrades them so low as not to leave them even a thought or desire of bettering their condition. But nature has long prepared a remedy for such great evils, in that unsubmitting, unconquerable spirit, with which she has inspired the people of the north; and thus she made amends to the human race for all the calamities which, in other respects, the inroads of these nations and the overthrow of the Roman Empire produced.

"The great prerogative of Scandinavia (says the admirable author of the Spirit of Laws*), and what ought to recommend its inhabitants beyond every people upon earth, is, that they afforded the great resource to the liberty of Europe, that is, to almost all the liberty that is among men. The Goth Jornande, adds he, calls the

---

* Baron de Montesquieu (L'Esprit de Lois).

north of Europe the forge of mankind. I should rather call it the forge of those instruments which broke the fetters manufactured in the south. It was there those valiant nations were bred who left their native climes to destroy tyrants and slaves, and so to teach men that nature having made them equal, no reason could be assigned for their becoming dependent but their mutual happiness."

H. W. LONGFELLOW is an enthusiastic admirer of the Scandinavian languages. Of the Icelandic he says: "The Icelandic is as remarkable as the Anglo-Saxon for its abruptness, its obscurity and the boldness of its metaphors. Poets are called Songsmiths;—poetry, the Language of the Gods;—gold, the Daylight of Dwarfs;—the heavens, the Scull of Ymer;—the rainbow, the Bridge of the Gods;—a battle, a Bath of Blood, the Hail of Odin, the Meeting of Shields;—the tongue, the Sword of Words;—river, the Sweat of Earth, the Blood of the Valleys;—arrows, the Daughters of Misfortune, the Hailstones of Helmets;—the earth, the Vessel that floats on the Ages;—the sea, the Field of Pirates;—a ship, the Skate of Pirates, the Horse of the Waves. The ancient Skald (Bard) smote the strings of his harp with as bold a hand as the Berserk smote his foe. When heroes fell in battle he sang to them in his Drapa, or death-song, that they had gone to drink 'divine mead in the secure and tranquil palaces of the gods' in that Valhalla upon whose walls stood the watchman Heimdal, whose ear was so acute that he could hear the grass grow in the meadows of earth, and the wool on the backs of sheep. He lived in a credulous age; in the dim twilight of the past. He was

"'The sky-lark in the dawn of years,
The poet of the morn.'

In the vast solitudes around him, the heart of Nature beat against his own. From the midnight gloom of groves; the deep-voiced pines answered the deeper-voiced and neighboring sea. To his ear, these were not the voices of dead, but living things. Demons rode the ocean like a weary steed, and the gigantic pines flapped their sounding wings to smite the spirit of the storm.

"Still wilder and fiercer were these influences of Nature in desolate Iceland, than on the mainland of Scandinavia. Fields of lava, icebergs, geysers, and volcanoes were familiar sights. When the long winter came, and the snowy Heckla roared through the sunless air, and the flames of the Northern Aurora flashed along the sky, like phantoms from Valhalla, the soul of the poet was filled with images of terror and dismay. He bewailed the death of Baldur, the sun; and saw in each eclipse the horrid form of the wolf, Managamer, who swallowed the moon and stained the sky with blood."

Professor W. FISKE, of Cornell University, who is undoubtedly the most learned northern scholar in this country, who has spent several years in the Scandinavian countries, and who is an enthusiastic admirer of Iceland and its Sagas, has sent me the following lines for insertion in this appendix:

"It is not necessary to dwell on the value of Icelandic to those who desire to investigate the early history of the Teutonic race. The religious belief of our remote ancestors, and very many of their primitive legal and social customs, some of which still influence the daily life of the people, find their clearest and often their only elucidation in the so-called *Eddic* and *Scaldic* lays, and in the Sagas. The same writings form the sole sources of Scandinavian history before the fourteenth century, and they not infrequently shed a welcome ray on the obscure annals of the British Islands, and of several continental nations. They furnish, moreover, an almost unique example of a modern literature which is completely indigenous. The old Icelandic literature, which Möbius truly characterises as 'ein Phänomen vom Standpunkte der allgemeinen Cultur und Literaturgeschichte,' and beside which the literatures of all the other early Teutonic dialects — Gothic, Old High German, Saxon, Frisian, and Anglo-Saxon — are as a drop to a bucket of water, developed itself out of the actual life of the people under little or no extraneous influence. In this respect it deserves the careful study of every student of letters. For the English-speaking races especially there is nowhere, so near home, a field promising to the scholar so rich a harvest. The few translations, or attempted translations, which are to be found in English, give merely a faint idea of the treasures of antique wisdom and sublime poetry which exist in the Eddic lays, or of the quaint simplicity, dramatic action, and striking realism which characterize the historical Sagas. Nor is the modern literature of the language, with its rich and abundant stores of folk-lore, unworthy of regard."

Benjamin Lossing says: "It is back to the Norwegian Vikings we must look for the hardiest elements of progress in the United States."

B. F. De Costa.—"Let us remember that in vindicating the Northmen we honor those who not only give us the first knowledge possessed of the American continent, but to whom we are indebted for much besides that we esteem valuable. For we fable in a great measure when we speak of our Saxon inheritance; it is rather from the Northmen that we have derived our vital energy, our freedom of thought, and, in a measure that we do not yet suspect, our strength of speech. Yet, happily, the people are fast becoming conscious of their indebtedness; so that it is to be hoped, that the time is not far distant when the Northmen may be recognized in their right, social, political and literary characters, and at the same time, as navigators, assume their true position in the Pre-Columbian Discovery of America.

"The twelfth century was an era of great literary activity in Iceland, and the century following showed the same zeal. Finally Iceland possessed a body of prose literature superior in quantity and value to that of any other modern nation of its time. Indeed the natives of Europe at this period had no prose literature in any modern language spoken by the people.

"Yet while other nations were without a literature, the intellect of Iceland was in active exercise, and works were produced like the Eddas and Heimskringla, works which, being inspired by a lofty genius, will rank with the writings of Homer and Herodotus while time itself endures."

Says Sir Edmund Head, in regard to the Norwegian literature of the *twelfth* century: "No doubt there were translations in Anglo-Saxon from the Latin, by Alfred, of an earlier date, but there was in truth no vernacular literature. I cannot name," he says, "any work in high or low German *prose*, which can be carried back to this period. In France, prose writing cannot be said to have begun before the time of Villehardouin (1204) and Joinville (1202); Castilian prose certainly did not begin before the time of Alfonso X (1252); Don Juan Manvel, the author of *Conde Lucanor*, was not born till 1282. The *Cronica General de Espana* was not composed till at least the middle of the thirteenth century. About the same time the language of Italy was acquiring that softness and strength, which were destined to appear so conspicuously in the prose of Boccaccio and the writers of the next century.

"Of course there was more or less poetry, yet poetry is something that is early developed among the rudest nations, while good *prose* tells that a people have become highly advanced in mental culture."

WILLIAM and MARY HOWITT.—"There is nothing besides the Bible, which sits in a divine tranquility of unapproachable nobility, like a King of Kings amongst all other books, and the poem of Homer itself, which can compare in all the elements of greatness with the Edda. There is a loftiness of stature, and a growth of muscle about it which no poets of the same race have ever since reached. The obscurity which hangs over some parts of it, like the deep shadows crouching mid the ruins of the past, is probably the result of delapidations; but amid this stand forth the boldest masses of intellectual masonry. We are astonished at the wisdom which is shaped into maxims, and at the tempestuous strength of passions to which all modern emotions appear puny and constrained. Amid the bright sunlight of a far-off time, surrounded by the densest shadows of forgotten ages, we come at once into the midst of gods and heroes, goddesses and fair women, giants and dwarfs, moving about in a world of wonderful construction, unlike any other worlds or creations which God has founded or man has imagined, but still beautiful beyond conception.

"The Icelandic poems have no parallel in all the treasures of ancient literature. They are the expressions of the souls of poets existing in the primeval and uneffeminated earth. They are limnings of men and women of godlike beauty and endowments, full of the vigor of simple but impetuous natures. There are gigantic proportions about them. There are great and overwhelming tragedies in them, to which those of Greece only present any parallels.

"The Edda is a structure of that grandeur and importance, that it deserves to be far better known to us generally, than it is. The spirit in it is sublime and colossal."

PLINY MILES. — "The literary history of Iceland in the early ages of the Republic, is of a most interesting character. When we consider the limited population of the country, and the many disadvantages under which they labored, *their literature is the most remarkable on record.* The old Icelanders, from the tenth to the sixteenth century, through a period of the history of the world when little intellectual light beamed from the surrounding nations, were as devoted and ardent workers in the fields of history and poetry as any community in the world under the most favorable circumstances. Springing from the old Norse or Norwegian stock, they carried the language and habits of their ancestors with them to their highland home. Though a *very large* number of our English words are derived direct from the Icelandic, yet the most learned and indefatigable of our lexicographers, both in England and America, have acknowledged their ignorance of this language.

"The Eddas abound in mythological machinery to an extent quite equal to the writings of Homer and Virgil."

The learned German writer SCHLEGEL, in his "Esthetics and Miscellaneous Works," says: "If any monument of the primitive northern world deserves a place amongst the earlier remains of the south, the Icelandic Edda must be deemed worthy of that distinction. The spiritual veneration for Nature, to which the sensual Greek was an entire stranger, gushes forth in the mysterious language and prophetic traditions of the Northern Edda with a full tide of enthusiasm and inspiration sufficient to endure for centuries, and to supply a whole race of future bards and poets with a precious and animating elixir. The vivid delineations, the rich glowing abundance and animation of the Homeric pictures of the world, are not more decidedly superior to the misty scenes and shadowy forms of Ossian, *than the Northern Edda is in its sublimity* to the works of Hesiod."

PROF. DR. DIETRICH asserts "that the Scandinavian literature is *extraordinarily* rich in all kinds of writings."

HON. GEORGE P. MARSH.—"It must suffice to remark that, in the opinion of those most competent to judge, the Icelandic literature has never been surpassed, if equaled, in all that gives value to that portion of history which consists of spirited delineations of character and faithful and lively pictures of events among nations in a rude state of society.

"That the study of the Old-Northern tongue may have an important bearing on English grammar and etymology, will be obvious, when it is known that the Icelandic is most closely allied to the Anglo-Saxon, of which so few monuments are extant; and a slight examination of its structure and remarkable syntactical character will satisfy the reader that it may well deserve the attention of the philologist."

The excellent writer, CHARLES L. BRACE, in speaking of Iceland, says: "The Congress, or 'Althing,' of the Icelanders, had many of the best political features which have distinguished parliamentary government in all branches of the Teutonic race since. Every freeholder voted in it, and its decisions governed all inferior courts. It tried the lesser magistrates, and chose the presiding officers of the colony.

"To this remote island (Iceland) came, too, that remarkable profession, who were at once the poets, historians, genealogists and moralists of the Norse race, the Scalds. These men, before writing was much in use, handed down by memory, in familiar and often alliterative poetry, the names and deeds of the brave Norsemen, their victories on every coast of Europe, their histories and passions, and wild deaths, their family ties, and the boundaries of their possessions, their adventures and voyages, and even their law and their mythology. In fact, all that history and legal documents, and genealogical records and poetry transmit now, was handed down by these bards of the Norsemen. Iceland became their peculiar center and home. Here, in bold and vivid language, they recorded in works, which posterity will never let die, the achievements of the Vikings, *the conquest of almost every people in Europe by these vigorous pirates;* their wild ventures, their contempt of pain and death, their absolute joy in danger, combat and difficulty. In these, the oldest records of *our* (*i. e.* the Americans') forefathers, will be found even among these wild rovers the respect for law which has characterized every branch of the Teutonic race since; *here, and not in the Swiss cantons, is the beginning of Parliament and Congress; here, and not with the Anglo-Saxons, is the foundation of trial by jury; and here, among their most ungoverned wassail, is that high reverence for woman, which has again come forth by inheritance among the Anglo-Norse Americans.* The ancestors (at least morally) of Raleigh and Nelson, and Kane and Farragut, appear in these records, among these sea-rovers, whose passion was danger and venture on the waters. Here, too, among such men as the 'Raven Floki,' is the prototype of those American pioneers who follow the wild birds into pathless wildernesses to found new Republics. *And it is the Norse "udal" property, not the European feudal property, which is the model for the American descendants of the ancient Norsemen.*

"In these Icelandic Sagas, too, is portrayed the deep moral sentiment which characterizes the most ancient mythology of the Teutonic races. Here we have no dissolute Pantheon, with gods reveling eternally in earthly vices, and the evils and wrongs of humanity continued forever. Even the ghosts of the Northmen have the muscle of the race; they are no pale shadows flitting through the Orcus. The dead fight and eat with the vigor of the living. But there comes a dread time, when destiny overtakes all, both human and divine beings, and the universe with its evil and wrong must perish (Ragnarokr). Yet even the crack of doom finds not the Norsemen timid or fearing. Gods and men die in the heat of the conflict; and there survives alone, Baldur, the "God of Love," who shall create a new heaven and a new earth.

"It is from Iceland that we get the wonderful poetic and mythologic collections of the 'Elder' and 'Younger Edda.' In this remote island the original Norse language was preserved more purely than it was in Norway or Denmark, and the Icelandic literature shed a flood of light over a dark and barbarous age. Even now the modern Icelanders can read or repeat their most ancient Sagas with but little change of dialect.

"But to an *American*, one of the most interesting gifts of Iceland to the world is the record of the discovery of Northern America by Icelandic rovers (?) near the year 1000.

"We think few scholars can carefully read these Sagas, and the accompanying in regard to Greenland, without a conviction that the Icelandic and Norwegian Vikings did at that early period discover and land on the coast of our Eastern States. * * * * The shortest winter day is stated with such precision as to fix the latitude near the coast of Massachusetts and Rhode Island. * * * * Iceland, then, has the honor of having discovered America.

"That volcano-raised island, with its mountains of ice and valleys of lava and ashes, has played no mean part in the world's history."—*Christian Union, July 15, 1874.*

The famous GEORGE STEPHENS, in his elaborate work on "Runic Monuments," having discussed the importance of studying the Scandinavian languages in order that many of our fine old roots may again creep into circulation, says: "Let *us* (the English) study the Scandinavian languages, and ennoble and restore our mother tongue. Let the Scandinavians study Old English as well as their own ancient records, give up mere provincial views, and melt their various dialects into one shining, rich, sweet and manly speech, as we have done in England. Their High Northern shall then live forever, the home language of eight millions of hardy freemen, our brothers in the east sea, our Warings and Guardsmen against the grasping clutches of the modern Hun and the modern Vandal. The time may come when the kingdom of *Canute* may be restored in a nobler shape, when the bands of Sea-kings shall rally round one Northern Union standard, when one *scepter* shall sway the seas and coasts of our forefathers from the Thames to the North Cape, from Finland to the Eider.

"We have watered our mother tongue long enough with bastard Latin; let us now brace and steel it with the life-water of our own sweet and soft and rich and shining and clear ringing and manly and world-ranging, ever dearest ENGLISH!"

In his preface to his Icelandic grammar, Dr. G. W. DASENT says: "Putting aside the study of Old Norse for the sake of its magnificent literature, and considering it merely as an accessory help for the English student, we shall find it of immense advantage, not only in tracing the rise of words and idioms, but still more in clearing up many dark points in our early history; in fact, so highly do I value it in this respect, that I cannot imagine it possible to write a satisfactory history of the Anglo-Saxon period without a thorough knowledge of the Old Norse Literature."

DR. DASENT, in his introduction to Cleasby's and Vigfusson's Icelandic Dictionary, says of Iceland: "No other country in Europe possesses an ancient vernacular to be compared with this." And again: "Whether in a literary or in a philological point of view, no literature in Europe in the middle ages can compete in interest with that of Iceland. It is not certainly *in forma pauperis* that she appears at the tribunal of learning." In another place he remarks: "In it (the Dictionary) the English student now possesses a key to that rich store of knowledge which the early literature of Iceland possesses. He may read the Eddas and Sagas, which contain sources of delight and treasures of learning such as no other language but that of Iceland possesses."

The distinguished German scholar, ETTMÜLLER, in comparing the literature of the Anglo-Saxons with that of the Icelanders, says: "Neither the Goths, nor the Germans, nor the French can be compared with the Anglo-Saxons in the cultivation of letters. By the *Scandinavians alone*, they are not only equaled, but also surpassed in literature." And again: "If the Scandinavians excel in lyric poetry, the Anglo-Saxons can boast of their epic poetry. If the famous island in the remote northern sea applied itself with distinguished honor to historical studies, the isle of the Anglo-Saxons is especially entitled to praise from the fact that it produced orators, who, considering the time in which they lived, were decidedly excellent."

MAX MÜLLER, in his "Science of Language," says: "There is a third stream of Teutonic speech, which it would be impossible to place in any but a co-ordinate position with regard to Gothic, Low and High German. This is the *Scandinavian* branch."

In WHEATON's "History of the Northmen," we find the following passages: "The Icelanders cherished and cultivated the language and literature of their ancestors with remarkable success. * * * * In Iceland an independent literature grew up, flourished, and was brought to a certain degree of perfection *before the revival of learning in the south of Europe.*"

ROBERT BUCHANAN, the eminent English writer, in reviewing the modern Scandinavian literature, says: "While German literature darkens under the malignant star of Deutschthum, while French art, sickening of its long disease, crawls like a leper through the light and wholesome world, while all over the European continent one wan influence or another asserts its despair-engendering sway over books and men, whither shall a bewildered student fly for one deep breath of pure air and wholesome ozone? Goethe and Heine have sung their best — and worst; Alfred de Musset is dead, and Victor Hugo is turned politician. Grillparzer is still a mystery, thanks partly to the darkening medium of Carlyle's hostile criticism. From the ashes of Teutonic transcendentalism rises Wagner like a Phœnix,— a bird too uncommon for ordinary comprehension, but to all intents and purposes an anomaly at best. One tires of anomalies, one sickens of politics, one shudders at the petticoat literature first created at Weimar; and looking east and west, ranging with a true invalid's hunger the literary horizon, one searches for something more natural, for some form of indigenous and unadorned loveliness, wherewith to fleet the time pleasantly, as they did in the golden world.

"That something may be found without traveling very far. Turn northward, in the footsteps of Teufelsdrochk, traversing the great valleys of Scandinavia, and not halting until, like the philosopher, you look upon 'that slowly heaving Polar Ocean, over which in the utmost north the great sun hangs low.' Quiet and peaceful lies Norway yet as in the world's morning. The flocks of summer tourists alight upon her shores, and scatter themselves to their numberless stations, without disturbing the peaceful serenity of her social life. * * * The government is a virtual democracy, such as would gladden the heart of Gambetta, the Swedish monarch's rule over Norway being merely titular. There are no hereditary nobles. There is no 'gag' on the press. Science and poetry alike flourish on this free soil. The science is grand as Nature herself, cosmic as well as microscopic. The poetry is fresh, light, and pellucid, worthy of the race and altogether free from Parisian taint."

"Björnstjerne Björnson,* one of the most eminent of living Norwegian authors, is something more than even the finest pastoral taleteller of this generation. He is a dramatist of extraordinary power. He does not possess the power of imaginative fancy shown by Wergeland† (in such pieces as *Jan van Huysums Blomsterstykke*), nor Welhaven's‡ refinement of phrase, nor the wild melodious abandon of his greatest rival, the author of *Peer Gyut*;‖ but, to my thinking at least, he stands as a poet in a far higher rank than any of these writers.

"In more than one respect, particularly in the loose, disjointed structure of the piece, '*Sigurd Slembe*' reminds one of Goethe's '*Goetz*,' but it deals with materials far harder to assimilate, and is on the whole a finer picture of romantic manners. Audhild (a prominent character in '*Sigurd Slembe*,') is a creation worthy of Goethe at his best; worthy, in my opinion, to rank with Clærchen, Marguerite, and Mignon, as a masterpiece of delicate characterization. And here I may observe, inci-

---

* Björnstjerne Björnson was born in 1832; has written several novels, dramas, and epic poems. "*Sigurd Slembe*" is a drama, published in 1863, of which Robert Buchanan says: "It is, besides being a masterpiece by its author, a drama of which any living European author might be justly proud." Several of his novels, including "Arne," "A Happy Boy," "The Fishermaiden," have been translated into English.

† Henrik Arnold Wergeland was born in 1808, and died in 1845. He is the *Byron* of the North. His works comprise nine ponderous volumes. He excelled in lyrics.

‡ John Sebastian Welhaven, born in 1807, died 1873. Remarkable for the elegance and chasteness of his style. No poet has more beautifully and correctly described the natural scenery of Norway.

‖ The author of "*Peer Gyut*" is Henrik Ibsen, born in 1828. Was engaged by Ole Bull as instructor at the theatre in Bergen, which position he occupied six years. He has written several dramatic works, chiefly of a polemic and exceedingly satirical nature. Many of his countrymen prefer Ibsen to Björnson. His last work is "*Keiser og Galilæer*."

dentally, that Bjornson excels in his pictures of delicate feminine types,— a proof, if proof were wanting, that he is worthy to take rank with the highest class of poetic creators."

I might add to the above quotations from Max Müller, the brothers Grimm and many other eminent writers; but in the first place this article is long enough, and in the next place the works of the last named authors are accessible to all who may wish to investigate this subject further. My object has been to show that, in the opinion of those who have studied the subject, the North has a history, language and literature deserving and amply rewarding some attention from American students. Of the good or ill performance of this task the reader, whom I earnestly request carefully to consider the contents of these pages, must be the judge.

PUBLISHED BY S. C. GRIGGS & CO., CHICAGO.

A LITERATURE OF A THOUSAND YEARS:
Now opening to the research of American Scholars.
RECENTLY PUBLISHED:

A Norwegian-Danish Grammar & Reader

With a Vocabulary, designed for American Students of the Norwegian-Danish Language.

BY REV. C. I. P. PETERSON,
Professor of Scandinavian Literature, and Member of the Chicago Academy of Sciences.

202 pages. — — — *Price, $1.25.*

TABLE OF CONTENTS.

I. GRAMMAR.

ORTHOGRAPHY,	11
ETYMOLOGY,	13
Articles,	13
Nouns,	13
Adjectives,	17
Numerals,	21
Pronouns,	22
Verbs,	25
Adverbs,	36
Prepositions,	36
Conjunctions,	37
Interjections,	37
SYNTAX,	38
IDIOMS,	44
PROVERBS,	52

II. READER.

HISTORICAL SKETCHES AND TALES.

Norway a Thousand Years Ago.	54
The Kings of Norway. *H. Wergeland,*	57
Rollo of Normandy. *S. Petersen.*	62
The Discovery of Iceland. *P. A. Munch,*	63
The Discovery of America by the Northmen. *D. Schoyen,*	66
A Legend about St. Olaf. *S. Welhaven,*	68
The Battle at Stanford Bridge. *S. Petersen,*	71
The Song of Sinclair. *E. Storm,*	73
The Union of N'w'y and Sweden,	76
Tale-Tellers. *J. Moe,*	78
Old Mother Margrethe at the Gate of Heaven. *H. C. Andersen,*	79
Canute the Great. *A. Oehlenschlæger,*	82
Navy Song. *Joh. Evald,*	85
Norwegian Flag Song. *C. N. Schwach,*	86
Patriotic Song. *B. Bjørnson,*	87

BIOGRAPHICAL SKETCHES.

Commemoration of Luther. *N. F. S. Grundtvig,*	89
King Christian IV. *F. Hammerich,*	91
Thomas Kingo. *M. Hammerich,*	92
Niels Juel,	95
Ludvig Holberg. *C. A. Thortsen,*	96
Peter Tordenskjold,	100
Hans Egede,	102
Bertel Thorvaldsen,	104
Adam Oehlenschlæger. *M. Hammerich,*	106
Christopher Hansteen,	109
Michael Sars,	110

SKETCHES FROM NATURE.

The Waters of Norway. *L. K. Daa,*	111
A Trip Across Norway. *The Author,*	114
The Midnight Sun. (Fr. Bayard Taylor's "Northern Travel,"	117
Herds of Reindeer in Finmarken. *N. V. Stockfleth,*	119
Ascension of the "Horsemen Mountain." *A. Vibe,*	123
Reindeer-Hunting on the "High Mountain." *P. Asbjørnsen,*	126
A Norwegian Patriotic Song. *S. O. Wolff,*	130
The Departure. *A. Munch,*	132
A Stranding on the West'n Coast of Jutland. *S. S. Blicher,*	133

III. VOCABULARY,	137
IV. Remarks on the History of the Norwegian-Danish Language,	192
V. Notes on the Authors from whom Selections have been made,	197 to 202

PUBLISHED BY S. C. GRIGGS & CO., CHICAGO.

WHAT IS SAID OF
PETERSON'S
Norwegian-Danish Grammar & Reader.

In my judgment the author has done himself much credit, and I trust his Grammar will be the means of inducing many Americans to study the Norwegian language, literature and history.—*Prof. R. B. Anderson, University of Wisconsin.*

I may say that I have myself read through the Norwegian-Danish Grammar of Peterson, and when I affirm that I find myself able to translate the reading exercises with great readiness, it may be inferred how well the book is adapted to forward one in a knowledge of this interesting but neglected language.—*A. Winchell, late Chancellor of the University of Syracuse, N. Y.*

Just what I want myself, and I believe that a great many others will tell you the same. The plan of the book is simple and judicious; the execution is excellent. The selections of the reader I should judge to be very happy. The author is much indebted to his publishers for the handsome dress of his work.—*Prof. William W. Folwell, President of the University of Minnesota.*

I rejoice to see the door opened to American students to the treasures of Norwegian letters, and in so attractive a manner as in Mr. Peterson's work. No more useful direction for philological study opens before English scholars now than the research into the Anglo-Saxon and Norse Northern tongues. This work will be surely a valuable help in this direction.—*Rev. Frank Sewell, President of Urbana University, Ohio.*

By the aid of this text-book one may find his way into the literary treasures of Norway and Denmark, which, although not great in numbers, have a great literature.—*Chicago Journal.*

The Scandinavian languages and literature are rapidly becoming of a like importance and value, to Americans, with the German. * * * The manual here offered to the public is an exceedingly convenient and serviceable one, comprising grammar, reader, and dictionary within the compass of one handy volume. To one who has some knowledge of German especially, and to any one in fact, it is a comparatively easy matter, with the aid of such a manual, to get a substantial foothold in this field of linguistic study.—*The Standard, Chicago.*

This little work fills a want which has long been felt. The throngs of incoming Scandinavian immigrants, who are yearly adding to the swarms already here, will soon make the Norwegian-Danish tongue as important an element in business and life as the German is at the present. * * Irrespective of the practical usefulness of the acquisition of the Norwegian-Danish tongue, its wealth of literature cannot fail to make it an object of the deepest interest to the scholar and the man of culture. It cannot be doubted that Mr. Peterson has in this little text-book made a genuine addition of not a little importance to the literature of schools, which will result in widespread benefit.—*Chicago Times.*

Sent, postage paid, on receipt of $1.25 by

S. C. GRIGGS & CO.,
Publishers, CHICAGO.

www.ingramcontent.com/pod-product-compliance
Lightning Source LLC
Chambersburg PA
CBHW022147160426
43197CB00009B/1465